The Rhizome as a

Field of Broken Bones

D1565657

The Rhizome as a

Field of Broken Bones

new poems

Margaret Randall

WingsPress

San Antonio, TX

2013

The Rhizome as a Field of Broken Bones
© 2013 by Margaret Randall

Cover: *Molecular Image* © 1975 by Rini Price.

First Edition

Print Edition ISBN: 978-1-60940-285-3
ePub ISBN: 978-1-60940-274-7
Kindle ISBN: 978-1-60940-275-4
PDF ISBN: 978-1-60940-276-1

Wings Press
627 E. Guenther
San Antonio, Texas 78210
Phone/fax: (210) 271-7805

On-line catalogue and ordering:
www.wingspress.com
All Wings Press titles are distributed to the trade by
Independent Publishers Group
www.ipgbook.com

Library of Congress Cataloging-in-Publication Data:

Randall, Margaret, 1936-
  [Poems. Selections]
  The rhizome as a field of broken bones : new poems /
Margaret Randall. -- First edition.
      pages cm
  ISBN 978-1-60940-285-3 (pbk. : alk. paper) -- ISBN
978-1-60940-274-7 (epub ebook) -- ISBN 978-1-
60940-275-4 (kindle ebook) -- ISBN 978-1-60940-
276-1 (library pdf ebook)
  I. Title.
  PS3535.A56277R48 2013
  811'.54--dc23
                              2012045811

This book is for V. B. Price, poet, friend.

Contents

The Rhizome as a

Field of Broken Bones

The Rhizome as a Field of Broken Bones

From hops to orchids,
ginger to the sanctified bloom
we call Lily of the Valley
a horizontal stem
or root mass
moves beneath the ground,
feeling its way,
choosing where it will wake and rise
in yet another multiplying mirror
we hold to history.

The ancient Greeks gave us
this anatomy: rhizome
as key to vegetable resistance.
Utah's Pando colony
of Quaking Aspen
a million years young.
Neither foragers, insects,
fungus nor fire
shatters the design
of its secret hiding place.

At this level of our fractal universe
elegant fern
and plebian Bermuda grass,
purple nut sedge
or obstinate poison oak
wait at trail edge
for the next hiker's
bare legs:
all speak the language of rhizome
to our grateful ears.

We who see a field
of broken bones
view pale faces
on memory's imprint
befriend the rhizome:
neither beginning nor end.
Balanced at midpoint,
it resists chronology
and we claim our place
as nomads on a savage map of risk.

Not linear narrative but radiant grid
where four dimensional images dance
and one rain forest butterfly
bloats a Kansas funnel cloud
with energy unmeasured
by the lab scientist
willing to consider
a million lives collateral damage,
intent only on his chance
at the big prize.

Imagine you are a child
in Phnom Penh,
the skulls creeping rootstalks,
one sprouting another
from its node
of ideology gone insane,
twenty sprouting a thousand,
two million, a landscape
where above ground and below
a single terror moves.

Pull your only legacy back
through Treblinka's classrooms
where desperate teachers
help children wrap memory

paint freedom
on comforting squares of paper.
Wander among piles of shoes,
mountains of human hair,
each new node
an evil birthing.

Rest yourself in phantom Elazig,
now Turkey in denial,
where thousands of Armenians
lived and loved
before the genocide.
Contemplate the sharp edge
of a Rwandan machete
and try to remember if you
wielded the weapon or knew its steel
against your throat.

Enter this complex community
through its back door,
breach its rockiest border
and break the hold
steep systems of convention
have on you.
Open yourself to time
in every dimension.
Welcome a new home.

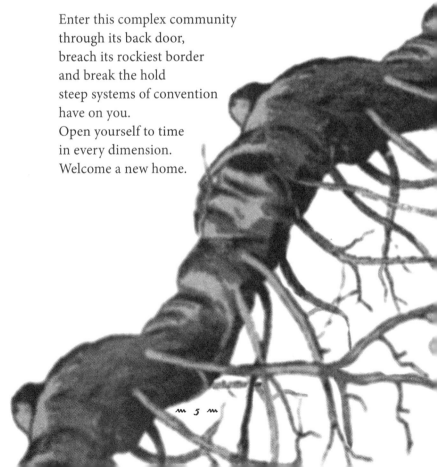

Today I am one more
body of water
filling available space,
trickling down
through fissure and gap
toward a new map,
eroding what stands in my way.
You may try to interrupt my dance
but your ugly language
leaves no signature.

La Llorona

It should come as no surprise.
I found her
by the banks of the San Antonio.
I know, you'd think she'd choose
the Rio Grande or Colorado
for her nightly walks:
rivers of strength and purpose,
dividing nations or raging
through the greatest canyon of them all.
But I knew
she preferred more intimate beauty.
I'd done my homework.

I almost didn't hear her whispered wail
between the moan of freight trains
charging night
in that south Texas city.
I thought I discerned a minor key,
high harmony in late September
and followed the sound
notebook in hand,
sharpened pencil ready.

Around the bend she sat alone,
magnificent profile
hidden beneath her long black veil
I confused at first
with tree shadows in quiet air.
Almost midnight,
still high nineties.
Who could sleep?
I thought she might run
but she turned

slowly toward me,
seemed resigned to talk.

Gain her confidence: oral historian's trick
before sympathy heated my blood
and for one brief moment
I felt what she felt
so many centuries before.
Do you mind if I sit, I trembled,
and she gave me to understand
scorn is a lonely companion,
she'd like the company.
Even legends
endure mistaken identity.

Fearful she'd fade in this Texas heat
I opened with the questions
I knew my readers wanted answers to:
Were you poor but beautiful?
Rich but ugly?
Or did you embody some other mix
of class and magnetism?
Did he come from afar
or was he someone
you played with as a child? You know,
before the era's gender roles kept you apart?

And, I took a breath, *let's talk*
about the children
—I know it must still be painful—
but there's no getting around it,
people want to know.
Did you drown them yourself
or was it someone else
pinned the crime on you?
Their father? Some other authority?

I knew I was breaking every journalistic rule
of free-world impartiality,
feeding questions,
imposing twenty-first century assumption
on this seventeenth century woman
who raised one slender hand
and brushed her veil aside.
A full moon infused her copper skin.
Eyes I'd expected puffy and red
pierced mine.

You've got to understand, she began,
her voice the rustle
of a thousand Sandhill Cranes,
we had few choices when I was alive.
It was marriage
or spend the rest of your days
serving father and brothers.
And yes, she leaned forward,
her face almost touching mine,
the rancid stench of wet leaves

penetrating my nostrils
as I steadied notebook,
struggled to breathe,
why keep it a secret after all this time:
my sort of beauty wasn't praised—
large nose and ears,
a few extra pounds,
fuzzy shadow smudging my upper lip,
eyes that saw too much.
I wanted out . . . no, no, erase that:
I had to escape or I'd have gone mad.

I know people say I was mad
but I was a woman with her life

and we didn't live long
back then,
one life I wasn't going to spend
with a man who only came home
tired of his latest fancy
and reeking of pulque,
how I recoiled at the sickening stench.

I loved my two little boys, of course I did,
Benjamín and Ceferino,
yes they had names
and I want you to name them,
all these years and no one's bothered to ask.
I loved my children and
I'll tell you now I tried to save them,
entered the river
though I couldn't swim,
struggled until water and reeds
threatened to pull me under,
watched the current carry their bodies away.

Why not proclaim my innocence?
I didn't expect that from you,
thought you smarter than to ask,
you must know we can talk and talk
and they still believe
only what fits the stories they write
to keep us under control.
Hysteric, they would have cried,
liar or worse.
Stories written long before my time
and I see nothing has changed that much.

Is that enough? She rose
and let the veil fall
across her dissolving face,
started to turn in resignation or disgust.
But maybe it was something in my eyes.
We were two women talking,
unperturbed by the distance
that separates her time from mine,
roles of historian and informant
long forgotten.

She offered one last smile
and I saw a glimmer
of sympathy
as if I was the twisted legend
and she the poet
destined to set the record straight.
Before she disappeared for good
among the oak and fruitless mahogany
she touched my hand.

Maybe in another hundred years, she said,
if our Mother hasn't devoured us all
and spit us back to space by then.

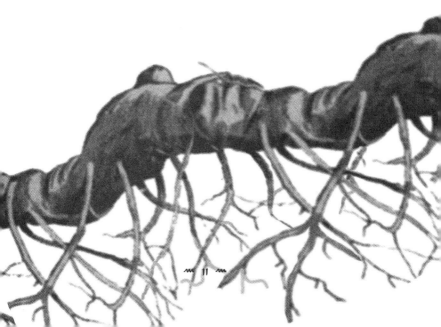

Canary in the Mine — 1

Chained to a School Board desk in Tucson, Arizona,
students protest the erasure of *In Lak Ech—*
You Are My Other Me.
Democracy beats them bloody.

Devious as Helen at Troy, Western Civ
and Last Supper pop-ups,
memory ancient as *maize*
and dangerous as who we know we are.

Following Nogales, Tucson, Chicago and north,
law becomes hate's trail of crumbs.
The walking dead climb aboard
an underground train of hope.

Dark ghosts breach borders rigged by men
on monumental steeds
who keep order
in the history we're taught.

Beyond the front-line border wall
invisible replicas fall like dominoes
across the next ridge and the next.
On the desert all the borders die.

Every brown child who fears questions,
papers, and the pale green *migra* van,
every child of every hue taught nothing
but how to score on the master's test,

marks time because thinking has turned
dangerous and living by the rules
foolproof prelude
to a future where none will hear the song.

When floodwaters recede and fire turns to ash,
when they come to see what's left
they will find a million dead canaries:
singing in perfect harmony.

Canary in the Mine — 2

In Dresden and Tokyo, Hiroshima, Baghdad,
Kabul, the Pine Tree Rez or South Bronx,
canaries are deemed collateral damage
by those who order the firepower, drop the bombs.

He comes from a war they said would keep us free.
Now home is a jigsaw puzzle with pieces missing.
No one can put it back together, no one
silence the waking dreams.

After two tours and a lie for every secret,
she thought the VA would help
but there's no place for women veterans with PTSD
and rape lives wherever healing turns a trick.

The latest in body armor leaves more amputees.
If there's anything left
send it back to a grateful nation
in the dignity of a flag-draped box.

For those who do come home: long silence,
beloved faces like no one she has ever known,
voices that tell her
she's the canary in the mine.

Canary in the Mine — 3

We turn the major battles over and over
in our hands
but ignore this man
who can't afford his final operation,
transgender skin folded, unfolded:
acceptable body armor.

Where male privilege falls short
some see a freak of nature,
others embrace identity's pride.
In this violent round
she/he's the latest canary in the mine.

Canary in the Mine — 4

A thousand feet beneath the African veld,
Atacama desert or gentle hills of Tennessee
ravaged lungs rasp a warning,
tell us miners themselves are the canaries in the mine.

On the highest catwalk of the tallest building
or locked inside a steel bullet on the ocean floor
I tell you all whose sweat turns instantly to blood
is tiny and yellow and sings:

every one of us: canaries in the mine.

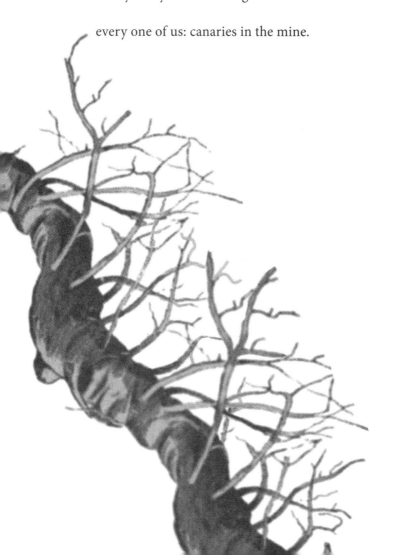

Wrong and Wrong

1

I boarded my first war train in 1942
when Dad sat one night at the edge of my bed,
faint scent of Old Spice and Army serge:
war as absence,
small tree of loneliness.

Too old for the draft and father of two
the Jew who spun his surname
in jump step with Mother's denial
but hated injustice,
heard the rumors, went to do his part,
fascism chewing at his Scarsdale collar.

For my generation this was The War
That Would End All Wars,
the good war no one challenged,
at least no one on that trusting terrain
where I waged my anxious childhood battles.

Grandpa's honeyed hands pulled me
into his *this is our little secret* war,
his *don't tell or I'll kill you* war,
the dreamy smile his deceptive weapon.

All these years later Dad's garrison cap
remains in my six-year-old hand
though I know he took it with him
to basic training at Fort Knox
and brought it with him on every furlough home.

From awkward accommodation
among recruits
better suited for the battlefield
through honorable discharge
and Tarrytown assembly line

where he came home from work one day
his arm a web of burnt flesh
hot metal against obstinate desire
resignation rising.

That war was Roger, my dog
they trained to kill
so couldn't send him back to a child
the official letter said.

Surprise blackouts, dark window shades,
ration cards and Bundles for Britain.
Clean your plate: you know
the children in Europe are starving.

Sudden wail of sirens and arms pressing
head into school desk
as if a child's posture could keep me safe.
Air raids strafing perfect lawns
each proud to do its part.

When tickertape finally filled the sky
we strutted past bedtime,
ran pajama-clad into victory-swollen streets
banged pans and celebrated righteousness,

a palpitation alternated neurons
and the young blonde woman
back arched beneath that sailor's
Times Square kiss,
never quite measured up in memory.

2

I missed Korea but went to Vietnam 1974,
and now I was in the field
though not a soldier
and not where patriotism wanted me.

Cuba to Paris, Paris to Moscow,
Moscow to Tashkent, Rangoon,
Vientiane and onto Hanoi:
flowers of greeting
women wearing white headbands
of white hot grief.

It was six months before the end of a war
that devoured three million Vietnamese
and 58,000 Americans not counting
those who succumbed to Agent Orange
suicide and madness.

The war we lost, the one that left
a nation divided, raw,
the one our history books
call Vietnamese
and theirs American.

I had to show up to understand
Vietnam was a country, not a war,
travel its narrow backbone
down Highway One
cross broad rivers where bridges

bombed for the twentieth time
became pontoon barges overnight
alive with people
who welcomed me with a smile,
flash of pain exploding in their eyes.

I went to meet an enemy
who was not my enemy,
listen to young peasant women
tell how they stretched their third-grade math
to bring the American bombers down.

How they entered tunnels where villagers
survived for years
cared for beloved water buffalo
even gave birth
and never doubted peace would come.

South of the 17th parallel
I bent to touch poisoned earth
where my government promised
nothing will grow for a thousand years,
learned courage would topple that promise.

3

Latin America's Dirty Wars caught me
on the ground in a decade
when orders were whispered
behind closed doors,
covert the name of every action.

We discovered the real meaning
of democracy then:
denial as code for
international treaties don't mean us,
torture a necessity and execution without trial
pride of The American Century.

I walked through battlefields
of Nicaraguan dead,

made the rounds to protect my neighborhood
through moist nights
watched my teenage daughters prepare for war.

I photographed the broken faces
of children in cheap coffins
wrote and published the news
my country kept from its headlines
made love and children and poems.

In Guatemala, Argentina and Uruguay
disappearance was the new weapon:
generations plucked one by one
from bedrooms and streets,
here one day, gone the next.

Those who survived might come home
with fangs implanted, mouths deformed
as message meant to warn anyone
daring to take their place.

4

In the same backrooms, refurbished now,
over brandy or whiskey
or a line of coke
men reeking with power
catch sight of sun on desert walls,
lust for their Seven Cities of Gold.

War wins only itself, eternally,
while a president
who promises to stop the slaughter
wages another
then wins the big Peace Prize.

One day this language of lies
will fall on its own bayonet.
In Iraq, Afghanistan, Libya
or wherever the bully takes us next.

The Lie keeps shouting
have to finish what we started
right or wrong
while every drumbeat heartbeat life beat
pulses wrong and wrong.

Coda:

Have I forgotten the silenced wars,
Armenia's genocide
or Cambodia's Killing Fields,
once so urgent in the news?
Should I have said Rwanda?

Can I really salvage our gentle memories
set in the wrong direction,
bloodied, gutted,
tripping over themselves
as they drag us to this sad farewell?

Tenderness is not collateral damage,
partial lines scrawled across a page
found among the ruins
of all our lives.

Our Job was to Move their Bodies

—for Daisy Zamora

1
Sometimes in the high noon heat of an August day,
monsoon rains coax millennia
of discreet scents
to the surface of my desert home.

Through layers of ancient cook pot smoke
smell of bone dreams and builds
bedrock to today's exhaling sage
and I catch that purging pungency.

Nineteen-seventy-nine and the war was won
or so we thought.
Along shell-pocked roads and small backyards
fallen revolutionaries outgrew their shallow graves.

Our job was to move their bodies
to proper sites, cemeteries
where a nation of lovers
could mourn them in gratitude.

What remained of red and black, one arm
of a checked shirt, a single shoe
or blood-caked pair of pants
now forever sizes large.
A skull came free in my hands.
Thin book of poems without a cover.

It was the stench that trapped us
where we worked,
invaded willing shovels
entered living nostrils
beneath protective safety masks.

I wondered how long before earth would calm
the clinging color of death.

But today I mourn a greater loss: pure scent
they fought for dunged by imposters,
murdered by power where every hack speech
every greed-spliced lie spits in the gaping sockets
of men and women
whose last sad fumes still gag my memory.

2
Faint olfactory waves at Rome's arenas
where clawed gladiator flesh
screams bloodied concession for the ages.
Unmistakable stench of human burning
no neighbor German farmer dared challenge.

Defining scent of death trapped on the surface
of an old black and white photo,
sight fading to smell when senses cross clean lines,
explode nerve endings,
render every explanation meaningless,
too messy to fold and file in neat drawers.

One unexpected unforgiving moment
always escapes the polished surface
of *we must never forget*
or *let's put it behind us and start again.*
Its rising mist menaces us where we stand.

Clean Red and Black

I had to look somewhere so fixed my eyes
on the mother's blue satin blouse,
one side of its collar pulled to the side
baring the starkness of breastbone and loss.

Strands of damp hair repeated their fall
across lips silenced by bullets
made somewhere else.
The small room's heat,
lungs under siege.

Walls receded, then pressed against me.
Slowly, with purpose,
I brought my gaze to her son's face:
jaw wrapped in strips of gauze,
clean red and black around his neck.

As in so many grieving homes
before and since
I touched the mother's shoulder
raised my camera, got my shot.

We must tell the world, they insisted,
when I complained I can't
keep doing this. Can't. Won't.
The mothers wept and in my dreams
I fled the disappearing faces of my own children.

Sad body-shaped boxes follow me now:
endless parade of containers,
planks, and shrouds on Palestinian shoulders
or thronging the streets of Soweto, Morazán,
Aleppo, Juárez, Chicago.

We've told the world.
When will the world listen?

Angkor

I was dragging my feet, the heavy air
hummed with low chatter of Gibbons,
one with a baby clinging to its belly,
all diving for tourist handouts
laced with plastic danger.

Other tourists swirled about me
like gnats, their squeals
little darts piercing my eardrums,
sweat pungent as my own
as we groped around each other
in the heat of a narrow passageway.

Green plastic tarps got in the way
and every visitor with a camera
bent or crouched for the view
that obscured the blemish.
I thought Photoshop
then resignation.

I moved to a low wall where
I could sit a while,
do battle with years of expectation.
A Gibbon masturbated
inches to my left.

Years yearning to make it to this place
on the far side of my world,
gaze at these Buddha-covered towers
damaged by neglect and weather,
once targets for the Khmer Rouge,
now a concession
managed by Vietnamese.

I wanted the Angkor Wat of kings,
flourishing in the shadow of Kulen,
bustling and trading
along the shores of Tonle Sap,
radiating culture throughout a world
alive one thousand years ago.

I wanted to cross the broad moat
with no Styrofoam in the water,
join saffron-robed monks
and pilgrims from everywhere,
understand its movement
from Buddhist to Hindu and back again.

I wanted to feel its pulse beneath my skin
and thought of Ginsberg here in 1963,
the questions he asked
and answers he left us
in practice and in poem.

I raised my eyes above the familiar silhouette,
and followed the cheap arc
of a large hot air balloon,
its basket squirming with point 'n shoots
aimed at the scene below.

I marveled at bas-relief stories:
human gesture on faces
more alive than what the Egyptians carved
so many centuries before
or the symbolic petroglyphs
of my own Southwest.

I identified with those Khmer faces:
dancing women, men returning
from victory, animals and trees.

My ears welcomed
their unfamiliar tones.

At Angkor Thom
the Elephant Terrace stunned me,
long sculpted trunks
extending beyond
a deeply incised façade.

At Preah Palilay I was gripped
by great Strangler Figs
holding the temples together
as they tore them apart.
Their twisted branches
embraced my fierce desire.

But I was tired, the sun relentless
and all this carved beauty
depicted war and conquest,
royalty and slaves,
men playing their eternal game
with women as pawn and ornament.

At the edge of moist vision
outliers stood immobile
in a jungle of green.
Destruction rose on every side
until I walked the empty causeway

and entered Banteay Srei,
its inner courtyard
gave me miniature temples
of pink sandstone
dressed in gray-green lichen,
blackened in places,
polished smooth in others.

Its lintels and pediments carried me
on a mythical journey
to where I crossed the bridge
between today and then,
those who lived in this place
and the poet struggling to breathe.

The town that surrounded this temple
is gone
as settlements always vanish
from such sites:
continuity swallowed by vendors
hawking sugar palm sweets,
sticky rice steamed in bamboo.
A brother and sister
descended from those ancient Khmer
stare from their rickety bike.

At Banteay Srei longing melts
in my hands,
my thirst is quenched,
my hunger for connection
finds the peace it seeks.

Time disappears.
Something amorphous
takes its place
and only gratitude remains.

Ode to General Võ Nguyên Giáp

*(Born in the village of An Xá, Vietnam,
August 25, 1911)*

The General was 100 in August.
He dreams of slender rubber trees,
white sap dripping into small bowls,
halved gourds filling with currency
for school books and medicine,
everything his people deserve

after centuries of Chinese, Japanese,
French and Americans
claimed their bamboo and mangosteen,
rice paddies and water buffalo,
men and women
who keep on giving themselves
for independence and freedom.

The General fights no more.
Each morning he wakes
to converse with tiny birds and ghosts,
hears the dissonant chorus
of every voice, of every man and woman
fallen along that trail
strong as their nation's spine.
Light as air he enters the tunnels
remembering every victory and defeat.

Spirits of comrades come to tea
and to reminisce: Pham Van Dong,
Nguyen Thi Dinh and Brother Ho,
their faces young and smooth again
as when the dream sweated damp walls
of colonial prisons,

hid in strands of human hair
and woven baskets of promise.

The General remembers
how he vanquished
one invader after another,
and how it was necessary to speak of art,
encourage poetry and song:
weapons as great as the hidden jungle trap
or those miles of tunnels
beneath the invader's unsuspecting feet.

From his 1954 offensive against the French
through the making of a people's army
to the 1975 campaign
named for legendary Ho.
When McNamara met with his counterpart
long after their war was memory
Giap smiled as he explained
Tonkin had been a snag
in his adversary's imagination.

Now the old General battles a different enemy:
disregard for the earth and all her gifts.
After so much human loss,
grief and chemical insult,
he knows every inch of his recovering land
is sacred.

Chinese bauxite mines and reckless dams
threaten the integrity
of a nation that has suffered too much
to cater to foreign greed
or even to its own.

The General was 100 in August.
He still has his heart on the pulse
of his people, still wakes each morning
wise and grateful for the new day.

David and Goliath

Time rolls off high mesas,
thin sheets of alabaster
tough as desert varnish.
Fear rises
between breastbone and heart
claiming its right to jolt
with the minor key strains
of Vietnam's national anthem.

Time and the musical phrase
so distant from my culture
seem an unlikely pair
of migratory birds
and I toss bits of memory
across this Linus blanket
—gossamer-light yet hooked
on every unresolved reward.

Vietnam: David and Goliath
of my generation.
Every righteous struggle
against gods of greed and blame,
every woman used and abused
only because she is a woman,
every hungry child
frightened of home.

Cunning disguises itself as solace,
roads wander a map
until they stagger to the edges and fall
from this enormous game board.

Invisible slivers of ice
burrow beneath skin
that only wants to be caressed
at every tired hollow.

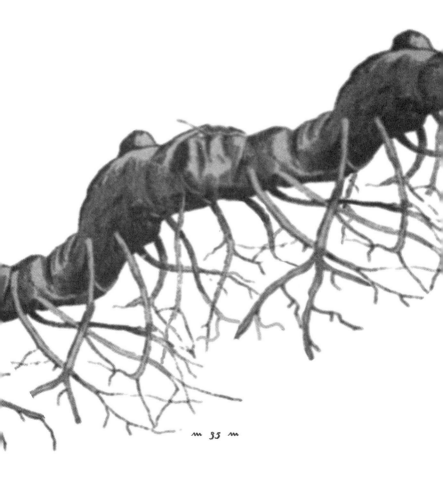

Writing on the Body

At Auschwitz seventy years ago
Yosef Diamant's Nazi captors
tattooed his forearm 157622.
Weapon of erasure
death blow to identity.

Some survivors hide their numbers
beneath long sleeves
revealing them only to lovers
averting their own eyes.
Others play them on the lottery.

All these years later, the fading digits
whisper horror, reduction, shame.
Writing on the body isn't always demolition.
It can be flag, eagle, naked woman
or indelible signature of love.

Initials, gang signs, drunken whim
or precious anniversary
also shout fidelity, control.
But whose fidelity?
Whose control?

Body writing: the torturer's hand
or memory's balm:
One badge of honor. One hideous scar.
Who writes
and who is written upon.

Today in a city where she hopes
terror can be kept at bay
Yosef's granddaughter Eli
shows him his numbers on her young flesh.
He bends to kiss the bridge of memory.

Intimately Defeated

Meditation on ex vice president
Dick Cheney's heart transplant.

He wakes with the new master muscle in place
but something is wrong.
Years of synchronizing heart and head,

the lust for power coursing through both
in syncopated symphony,
greed on the battlefield keeping perfect time

with corporate greed and the baton
he wields within his family
or on a friendly hunt.

He wakes and doesn't doubt
the transplant has been successful.
In every way but one.

No organ rejection or danger of infection,
no fever above his usual two degrees
below what other mortals know as normal.

This is a problem to baffle the specialists.
Maybe even
all of modern medicine.

Wife and daughters' smiles appear
through anesthetic haze:
they wouldn't understand

what he fears so he doesn't explain.
Vietnam. Halliburton. Iraq. Afghanistan.
Unwavering surveillance at home and abroad

drone into a disappearing distance.
None of five prior attacks
hinted at such dilemma.

The all-powerful man rests on white sheets.
State of the art equipment
hums and beeps about his bed.

Outside his hospital room
Secret Service best post serious guard
against the ever-lurking threat.

And the man who's always had an answer,
who's forever kept his razor-sharp cool,
wonders about the man

—or was it a woman?—
whose body only hours before
housed this heart now beating in him.

Could she have been a Democrat?
Could he have lost his job or home?
Or, god forbid, detested war?

Woman? Black? Lesbian? Transgender?
The anguished questions
course his veins:

ominous tide producing little stabs,
unfamiliar emotions he can't remember
experiencing before,

this strange irregular beat that has
rendered him physically sound at last
and intimately defeated.

True Grit of Old 66

In the steamy vortex between
First Street and Sixth
high-rise cluster of concrete
shrouds itself in colored light
to con the competition,
white stucco molding its undoing.

Grand Sunshine and dour El Rey
have parted company
from first-run glitter,
Skip Maisel is just a store these days.
Only the Kimo Theater
retains its whispered pomp.

Alvarado's ghostlike shadow
pushes through
the bus and train depot's faux facade
hoping to impress
when Rail Runner's red and yellow
bathe the station in commuter promise.

Is it the true grit of old 66 we need
to quicken our step
or a nod to today's reality
in a city where different
no longer clings
to the pages of a guidebook

and Indians from India buy Indian tacos
at the Pueblo Cultural Center
along with those who've lived here
centuries.

New neon
and pedestrian walkways

try hard to gentrify,
year after year
pull life back
from those All American malls
while shabby storefronts
don new masks.

But each Saturday morning in May
after sandstorms have settled
and heat climbs
its trickster scale,
a faint breeze moves
down Central Avenue

where the ghost of a young girl
—every desire yet to be granted
or withheld—
walks head thrust forward,
hands in pockets, eyes suspended
between a bleat of tears

and faded words on aging wind
cry: *Wait, wait, wait,*
here I come!

Only Swatch of Brown

—After "Nostalgia por la luz"
by Patricio Guzmán

Memory sinks its teeth into land so dry
it cannot shelter animals, plants
or moisture from distant snow.
Seen from space
Atacama is the only swatch of brown
on our blue and white sphere
spinning in the eternity of space.

Frigid nights, suffocating days,
brilliant moons:
memory loses its haunted way
crystalized in salt nuggets
and barren dreams.
Earth is broken into a patchwork
of hungry mouths.

Memory lives in the fingers
of a woman's dead hand
curled but reaching skyward
through captivity's pale green rope,
weave of a jacket still hugging her torso,
dusted surface of rock and sand
horizon to horizon.

Memory sounds in the wind-scoured ruins
of Chacabuco concentration camp
built over 19th century mining barracks
where men were slaves
and these prisoners worse than slaves.
Their families and this parched wood
remember.

Memory walks with the aging mothers
roaming this vast expanse,
fewer each season,
small orange beach shovels in their hands.
They move slowly, bend, retrieve
the smallest shard in cracked palms,
slip it into a shoulder bag, keep walking.

They are looking for evidence:
bone fragments among salt crystals,
pieces that can tell them
a son or daughter's life
ended on this desolate terrain.
Not dust to dust but calcium to calcium,
the stuff of stars, a living connection.

Thin Atacama air draws astronomers
with giant telescopes—
visual, radio—new pathways
retracing our enigmatic need to know:
where we began and how,
where we are going and what future
will hold a mirror to our past.

Cosmic archeologists say calcium,
material of stars and the human body,
builds us.
What we search for
across this desert
whose secrets shiver
through narrow canyons of escape.

Dry earth and thin air release twin truths
fourteen billion years
or four decades behind us
along with every story in between:

stories we resist
until they part the earth
and hit us where our knowing lives.

When we ask these questions
their answers demand
we follow their lead.
When we usher memory
into our porous lives
we run the risk of acknowledging
what it tells us of ourselves.

Every Equation Up for Grabs

Mesas stretch their purple fingers across sands
that offer withered *cholla* arms
in tentative embrace.

The monsoons are late this year and cactus aches
to plump green flesh with sustenance.
Dull blooms pale the exuberance

of wetter years. *Piñon* and sage sit staunch.
Yet the snow pack is high and deep
and as it melts

rivers rise above their banks.
Furious currents carve new *arroyos*,
rain arrives to save the *chile* crop.

North and east: sandbags cannot keep the water
from nuclear reactors.
One fear dominoes another.

A butterfly in North America gives birth
to a typhoon in Japan
but when nature on nature

gives way to human interference,
man against nature and man against man
every assumption stumbles,

every equation is up for grabs.

The Maze

Enter. Once you
have taken that first step
the rest is easy.
Well, perhaps not easy
but not as hard.

Don't raise your eyes
to walls of rock
old as earth itself,
cold as your three-year-old tibia
slashed from fibula

when everyone assured you
parents love their children
and every page of the Good Book
said this is life
as it's meant to be.

Greek flute condemned to silence.
Walls of jungle vine
impenetrable as forked tongues,
solid as this weight
pushing you down and out.

Look at your feet.
Journey left and right
in circles that hold you tight
and almost threaten
return.

Keep on walking so those in front
won't feel the wind of distance
at their backs
and those behind
may keep a human in the cross-hairs.

Do unto others, as the saying goes.
When your toes feel water rising
and you begin to hear
faint music of sea,
you will be invited to lift your arms,

reach out and touch this towering canyon
pulsing on either side.
Absorb the contour and meaning
of your path:
unidirectional yet woven of memory threads.

Its haunted colors shelter you
from pleasure and pain.
Twist your torso and say hello
to those nubby wings
as they sprout

from hunched shoulder blades.
Let loose.
Rise straight up
past pages torn from The Book,
from rock and ice and vine.

Free yourself from this maze
where the old lies
once pinned you
to a map drawn by imposters
and other creatures of hideous habit.

Mother Triptych

1

Supermarket neon claimed our neurons,
loss keeping you close to me
until you stopped:
Ginsberg's vision of Whitman
Old White Beard
among the vegetables.

You weren't Whitman but my mother.
I looked back and watched you lift
one ugly Portobello
by its thick stem,
your knobby hand clenched
just below its spreading threat of flesh.

Turning it slowly to your gaze,
perhaps wondering
why I am so afraid, perhaps knowing.
One aisle distant then
I swallowed memory trying to believe
you wouldn't move my way.

You put the mushroom back
pretended I hadn't seen
and we continued buying food
while I kept battering you
with small hurts, questions unanswered
before or since your death.

2

You asked about the big new County
Courthouse
bricks like sands of a desert we both love,
so many new buildings,
said you never noticed it before.

I told you we passed it every week,
maybe you don't remember,
strange pleasure of barbed words
only now echoing remorse.

Back then I wanted you to feel the shame
of memory loss
like images fallen beneath the waistband
of your old striped chambray skirt,

like your sad prosthetic breast
lodged there once on a walk
we took along Grand Canyon's rim,
Dad still with us, anguish in your eyes.

You didn't live to hear about the scandal
the senator who made millions
off that courthouse job,
didn't live to hear he's serving time:

the kind of news festooning
your shorter days
as more new buildings cut the skyline
of this city you wouldn't recognize.

3

We bought our little bags of mild green *chile*
at Sitchler's seasonal stand
a block from your Assisted Living,

until a guy in a white truck tall on super tires
blocked right then left and shrieked a menacing laugh
refusing to let us leave.

You sat small and silent when I opened my door
climbed from the driver's seat
and walked to his window

heart thundering, face on fire
steadying my voice
as I told him you were 96.

You're scaring my mother I said,
not you're scaring me,
then walked slow as I could

back to our car where I waited
for him to back up
and when he didn't

restarted my engine, inched around
his testosterone display
never taking my eyes from the ugly grin

and not once glancing at you, Mother,
holding your breath in the seat to my right
three years empty now.

Memory, It's Your Turn Now

Her lungs unfold—faint whisper
to those who, gazing
from our living heights,
gather round her bed—
then seize
and contract one last time.
All systems down.

Brief echo of twitching muscle,
tremor of body language:
intentional moments
and those she trailed in indecision,
imagining they might disappear
if she held her breath
or counted to herself.

The diary's tiny key no match
for any lock she's left behind,
the black box hides in sand
somewhere on an ocean floor.
True confessions
neither confessional nor true
in this aftermath of stalked desire.

Childhood house of forty rooms,
traveling salesman father
turned faith healer
with women everywhere
and lonely wife—petulance to poison—
complaining about a daughter
never good enough.

Choice of the good and patient husband
who only exploded once a year,
stayed despite her stream of lovers
or next exotic destination,
next lie that wished itself
to truth,
next imposter *mise en scène.*

The young doctor places her stethoscope
upon my mother's sunken sternum,
slightly right
of where her breast once was,
trained ears listen
for sounds from a map
unknown to me in every way but one.

We wait for the doctor
to lift the round disk,
move from the bed,
repack professional expertise
and pronounce the words:
time of death,
condolence or further instructions.

Life's meaning loosens the leather straps
climbing its ankles,
shifts weight from tired feet,
arranges itself on a wall of worn stone:
Etruscan, Roman, Greek,
and shouts in solid accent:
Memory, it's your turn now.

Daddy, Do You Remember Me?

Sixteen years and I can't conjure
your comforting hand
curled around mine,
your smell of Old Spice
set off by the temperature
you raised playing tennis
with neighbors half your age.

I can't evoke the name of the book
where you taught me to read
though its black letters on red pasteboard cover
still wander behind my eyes,
and I remember your serial tale
of Pufti and Mike, those picnics
where they chewed the drumsticks clean.

We rode the commuter train together
into the city when I was six.
You let me blend tobaccos in your tiny shop
and we broke Saltines in bowls
of Campbell's Alphabet Soup for lunch.
You taught me to swim and drive
and tell the truth.

Three years before you died we stood together
my angry fingers clasped in yours
—thick and protective—
one cold January night
on Albuquerque's Civic Plaza
protesting a war foreshadowing
others you wouldn't live to see.

When the confusion of age
shattered your knowledge base
your gentle nature
made the transition easy.
I was the parent now, you the child
whose muted wisdom
had finally come to rest.

Your strong body receded
into the nursing home bed,
eyes lost in diminishing sockets
until all I could do was say
I love you
and all you could give me in return
was *Ditto*.

Now the ashes remaining
from those we scattered
where you walked
your beloved German Shepherd
in mountains we made our home
sit in a cadmium red ceramic jar
here in this studio where I write.

Daddy, do you remember me?

Beneath Our Feet

—for Barbara

I will not use *sweetheart* or *forever*,
phrases like *meant to be* or other Hallmark lines
to describe what we discovered
that night of our perfect storm,
canyon wrens calling
down the arroyo that stopped
where time uncoiled at our feet.

Minutes swelled to hours and spirits
unburdened themselves of what they searched for.
Dreams and plenitude
breached prisons drawn by others.
Newly in possession of the recipe,
we were no longer the same
but so much more ourselves.

This happened to me once before
on a footbridge in Lima
when I walked into the arms
of a man I hardly knew,
but from the beginning we understood
ours would be a parenthesis,
finite as the perfect kiss on cracking celluloid.

A decade later we were two women
from different worlds,
mirrors reflecting unexpected images,
challenges we couldn't know in full,
so we placed our trust on the scales
and walked through embers
hot enough to banish doubt.

A quarter century later I touch
the definition of your arm, waist, thigh.
My older body still proud,
grateful to hold your lean strength
and unwavering commitment
in the still bright glow
of memory very slowly burning out.

Smuggled Our Side to Theirs

On the crumbling page of a broken photo album
highways of commerce
in the ancient city of Tenochtitlán
revive as floating gardens
nudging where I stand and why.

Destined invisible, small figure of a man
turns from the camera
as he poles his *Lupita*
through reeds
drowning small births and colorless deaths.

The camera is trained on five tourists
gathered by chance
who face its lens
beneath the gondola's blossoming arc.
I hear the *peso* changing hands.

That's my father seated right of the smiling group,
an unpaired woman beside him
and Mother center stage as always,
slightly parted teeth and closed lips
composed for the shutter's click.

Far left another couple completes the tableaux:
wife gripping her husband's arm,
his U.S. Army uniform sings duets
with the women's tailored suits
and low-heeled pumps.

Locals and tourists out for an afternoon
of south-of-the-border fun:
the scene is *Xochimilco,* year 1945
and our United States of America
has just won the War To End All Wars.

Dad joined despite his age, wanted
to do his part, flee the tensions at home.
Mother stayed 62 years,
a good husband, she said,
a good father.

Her words fought resignation,
great press of suffocating vines,
choked feeling,
keeping time to a music
born and bred in Scarsdale,

Albuquerque, or on that Mexican canal
where the happy group
floats in black and white
on the surface of this travel shot,
flanking the fifth woman who remains a mystery.

If I could pluck them from this faded surface,
I would grab their casual pose
until I too must cede the moment
to children or grandchildren
better equipped than I

to decipher such layers of deception,
stare down any camera lens
ready or not for today's *narco* wars
exploding in *corridos* of weaponry
smuggled our side to theirs in uniforms
emptied of all pride.

With Only Dirt

There's not much we can do with only dirt,
he says,
but we see he tries.

More than two hundred oval mounds,
some rimmed with small stones
or bearing whittled crosses

with dates when the bodies were found
on a desert
where mouths fill fast with sand.

Jane or John Doe, adult or child
the only identification
for those who carry neither name nor address,

whose families are too poor
to repatriate a body
from this journey's sudden end.

Downwind from Pecos

Downwind from Pecos, cedar scent
invades our nostrils,
transparent sky's unreachable blue

until this cloud that is not a cloud
but poison plume
rises imminent on horizon's shoulder,

reminding us Los Alamos is on fire
again
its people ordered to leave again

just as eleven years ago,
ordered to leave
in that orderly fashion,

lines of careful cars,
each keeping its distance
from the one in front.

Voracious cloud chews mountain ridge,
spews ash,
its bloated belly menacing orange glow.

Thirty thousand 55-gallon drums
of nuclear waste wait restive
as the flames advance and leap,

and other fatal chemicals
cross their fingers
in this game of Russian roulette.

Government spokesmen look directly
at the camera,
force eyes to focus, say there's nothing

to worry about: like Fukushima Daiichi
or Fort Calhoun
trembling on the banks of the rising Missouri,

before them Chernobyl and Three Mile Island:
each time-bomb
dressed in its reassuring lie

until blood drains from noses and ears
skin buckles
and internal organs trip over themselves

in their rush to an exit
whose door melts
before we can reach its threshold of deliverance.

At the Edges of the Pueblo

A great tree falls on a downed power line
and this time
the fire is dubbed accidental:
Cerro Grande, Las Conchas,

no resources spared in a month
of smoke-clogged sky
and the people of Los Alamos
finally breathe relief,

return to their homes, the threat
of that other accident
still raking memory,
PTSD common as the common cold.

To the southeast at Santa Clara,
beyond the Jémez
they drain two irrigation ponds
of water foul with dead fish.

The ditchwater in Hernández is also black
and plants grow slowly
thirsty for the nitrogen
that cowers in sweet-scented legends.

One burned elk comes into a garden
is about to speak
then falls and dies.
We wait for the wind to sing his funeral dirge.

One list holds the language of anxiety:
Oso Complex, Dry Lakes,
South Fork, Las Conchas, Cerro Grande.
Like broken thunder it overtakes

that other list: *Cochiti Mesa, Puye, P'opii Khanu.*
Turkey Girl is orphaned again
and gathers her starving charges
in secret canyons.

An ash cloud rises in air
we cannot breathe.
People say they saved Los Alamos
and let Santa Clara burn.

At the edges of the pueblo
all our ancestors weep.

All Maps Must Be Redrawn

Major highways dwindle
to narrower roads
then web into tractor ruts
and fading wildlife pathways
confuse themselves
with stretch marks: striations
marking the belly's rise
to embrace each child's coming.

A brushstroke of purple veins
climbs a new musical scale,
its ladder reaches bony shoulders,
cloak of arteries
clogged with decisions
that keep me awake
every night of my life.

Deep tracks mount one breast
then slowly circle the other's
well of unyielding loneliness.
A pull of years leads you
through the canyons of my jowl.
We labor to the end of a steep trail
that brings me home to myself
where you are waiting.

Canyon Ethnography

At least 2 billion years ago
this patch of earth's crust
opened its mouth and yawned,
lifted red walls off their haunches
and fed soft deltas
that would embrace community.

Today those prideful
of their brutalizing faith
stop at 4 thousand 5 hundred,
Noah's flood
and God's patriarch hand:
a single week of work.

Rainbow strata, fossils and
2 billion years of Vishnu Schist
undulate through the narrows
of this Inner Gorge.
230 million of Kaibab Limestone
hug the canyon rim.

Ancient seas advance, retreat
in silent recall.
Canyon cartography
implodes upon itself.
Evidence will always be
dogma to some, a map to others.

These Amazing Opposable Thumbs

So many ways to measure how we bloom
on this land we inherit
from ourselves:

how long we will have water, earth, trees,
veins of coal
coursing beneath our feet,

the air we breathe, sustenance and medicine
wrapping their delicate tendrils
about these amazing opposable thumbs.

Use or stewardship? Favoring the first
means sure death for the second.
Maybe our sense of balance

got kicked out of whack in the Garden,
maybe we never really
got it back.

Heat our homes and coat our lungs
in poison?
Harness the atom and vaporize

cities of children their first or only day
of school?
Get with the program

or do the simple math. This is when
it's time to admit:
where we are going

the canyon narrows to impenetrable rock,
trapping us in broken memory
we try but cannot escape.

I Suspect a Backup System

One billion Monarch butterflies
consult the sun's compass
then head south to Michoacán,

sated with milkweed pollen,
avoiding crazy corn
threatening larval mortality,

they are rich in the poison
that keeps them safe
from frogs and other predators.

Intuition leads the great migrations:
wildebeest and caribou
move toward new grass

but I suspect a backup system,
light-sensitive proteins
also script their grid.

Naval sonar confounds whales,
disappearing colonies of bees
take their honey with them.

Polynesian sailors sometimes
navigated 3,000 miles
under starless skies.

We too might have nurtured
the marker that would place us
in space but instead covet
instruments of progress,

bomb connective tissue
and every landmark
on our visual map is lost.

Civilization's magnetic field
finally pulls the switch on the sextant
once embedded in our cells.

Fetal

1

Shrunken, curled, imploded into disappearing
core,
fetal describes this place I inhabit,
distant from all previous space.

From the north: a cold so silent sound is not yet
born.
From the south; waves of decay,
steam rising beneath the body's trigger.

Eastern solutions don't fit or smell right,
won't satisfy a taste for blended spices,
groundswell of calendar stones.

West moves in too fast,
careens,
presses me in its ever-tightening vice.

One last hiss of breath
from lungs flattened to a single point
along horizon's gray-blue curve.

From above and below pressure takes aim,
hurtles into a heart that once believed
love conquers all.

2

Coiled in defeated mass of dying cells,
my 2012 instructions are:
wait. Try to sleep. Sleep and wait.

Something is happening:
nameless yet personal
and downwind from every directive.

Shrill exhortation and gentle plea
off-map from all those lines
gridded to show me the way.

3

One arm flies above my head,
extends in awkward angle
as it wakes from death.

A leg shoots out from my body,
finds no resistance,
continues its journey.

I hear my blood host images again,
warming muscle and skin,
making promises.

Faint Rorschach seeps through
delicate texture
of a Mobius strip

woven of perfect helix:
double, triple,
tethered to one elbow like a wing.

The active leg throws itself from bed,
seeks solid footing,
hits the floor running.

Arms extended, fingers take up the charge,
grab a pen,
begin to write.

Fetal, fetal again
but calling one last surprise
in this time of transient need.

When the Last Gulls Head for Shore

Sea perfect as glass or raging wild
masks hidden places:
canyon floors we cannot reach,
lives and treasure lost to a history
scattered in stories we know
and don't.

Tectonic plates crawl or heave
their restless shoulders,
volcanoes retch at depth
creating underwater Everests,
whirlpools more mysterious
than Bermuda's Triangle.

Iron links of an anchor chain
once coiled in pride
corrode beneath the dark of centuries.
Light gone out on regal crystal
leaves human sockets
empty.

Humpbacks launch their hopeful cries,
schools of dolphin leap
beside furrowing migration of ships
and dazzling blues and yellows
dart through lacey forests
of coral in foreclosure.

We cannot forget those mercury-
poisoned waters,
dead fish floating past demented sight,

atolls that were nations,
insignificant when measured
in foreign debt

and that one deceptive cloud
rising above the waves
or cursing their underside,
humanity's sad calling card
left again
and again.

Too late to lean out like a figurehead
at Titanic's prow
or fill my lungs with brine
when the last gulls
head for shore.
Too late to imagine
this is a game that will be won.

I am still aboard our battered ship,
tossed starboard and lee,
clinging to one demon-lashed rail,
gaining a surer footing
no longer my concern.
I wield my poor language

like a broken sextant, mesmerized
by the heave and pull of time
upon my history.
I weep for the stories lost
and a future that might have been
untethering at my waist.

Global Warming Danger #1

—for Eli Bickford

Walking on air, Manhattan's High Line
reconvenes old cargo tracks
flattened between modern tiling.
Native plants present their calling cards.

I no longer strain skyward
so every angle is new.
Its geometric altitude
flattens beneath my gaze.

I almost touch the old brick
of a warehouse to my left.
Geary's curves shimmer up ahead.
Signage inhabits my eyes on every side.

Weekenders stroll or sit, remove
shoes to cool their feet
in the glistening sheet of water
singing on stone beside us.

Where city stops, East River carries
my eyes to spar with this familiar skyline,
so used to telling us
there's nowhere to go but up.

This new angle on consciousness
surprises and comforts,
as if there is still hope,
as if it were not too late.

Three stories above the street,
you whisper: *Maybe*
it will escape the coastal flood.
Maybe it will be safe.

Evasive Poem

I wanted to write a poem,
pull one more ripple
of surprise from apron pocket,
dust off the stoneground flour
and smudge of butter,

replace their stains with a keyboard
of verbs, the perfect noun,
while sweeping
those pesky little prepositions
from my path.

No new idea stopped by
to say hello.
No unexamined angle
reached out to take my hand.
I felt anxious, bereft.

I slept badly last night and my dream,
patient even while it waited
for me to rouse myself,
grabbed hold again
once I returned to bed.

In the dream cold blue eyeballs
attacked from all sides,
granted no audience
but handed me a tiny Swiss Army knife
and cried *Peel me, peel me!*

As I carefully destroyed the surface
of each eye, another took its place
as cold as the one

exiting the picture frame,
dripping steely-blue tears.

Those eyes besieged me to wakefulness
and I've been immobile since,
unable to catch the poem.

Not Good News

I wanted to caress
relief
but this message
sets air on fire
knocks hope to the ground
raises a bitter churning
in my throat.

These words coat
the inside of my mouth,
my tongue,
unwilling to swallow,
bides time,
dislodges darts of fear and sadness
from between my teeth.

Teeth throb with certainty
of final approach
and by the way
that tangled weave of other deaths
forms a tightening web
on which my own years balance.

And by the way those distant deaths
from flood and famine
war and wandering,
women's bodies torn and strung
along our southern border,

Haitians who survived their earthquake
only to succumb to cholera,
miners giving up to greed,

those who know if they speak
they will die

and still they speak.
And by the way. And by the way.

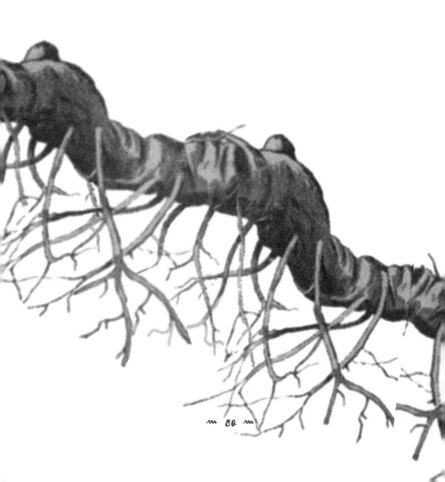

When I Grow Up

—for Tolo Bickford

When I grow up I want to be an old woman
unpredictable as a tornado
making landfall,
memory lightning sharp
for all those times
I played Elizabeth Taylor
caressed with violet eyes
the black horse or male lead,
desire in every sigh.

I want to remember
Athens' Golden Proportion
the Euphrates willowy banks
Petra's rosy light
and all the Serengeti's stars.

When I grow up I want
to be light as a feather
floating above a Nubian village
along the busy Nile,
a strong young woman
already sure
who I will be when I grow up.

Not Quite Blood

Not quite blood
but more than salt,
top tooth
into lower lip

bite just short
of breaking skin.
This is my
thinking hard

gesture, my
give me time
to get this right
device,

aimed at anyone
tempted to interrupt
or stand in the way
of halting progress

and well this side
of *you're done*:
senility's semaphore:
no more words at all.

The Human Privilege

Where the baboon tree holds males
in its highest branches,
females settle
a low line of defense
and babies cradle between.

Where sun warms the savannah
they all leap down,
chattering and grooming,
spend their days in community,
curious and fulfilled.

Where sibling wildebeest and zebra
run the Serengeti
to that place
of seasonal grass
before looping back

to where they live for each other
and birth their young:
one offers sight,
the other smell
in perfect choreography.

Where the wise lioness instructs
her daughters in the hunt
then, not driven by hunger,
veers away
inches before the lunge.

Where the ponderous elephant
draws sorrow
to a height of dignity
and stops to nuzzle
the bones of his lifelong friend.

Where the matriarch moves
in tandem with memory,
takes an old road home
and charges resolute
through whatever blocks her way.

Where whales braving sonar barricades
keen on the ocean floor
and a thousand miles distant
another great body
lifts and swims to keep the date.

They need no rules and gluttony
is not a virtue.
No one buys votes or lies about their opponent.
Here we claim with pride
discernment as the human privilege.

Misión San José

—for Bryce Milligan

Its always a toss up between admiring
those massive limestone walls,
Our Lady of Guadalupe
radiant in her star-studded cloak,

vaulted ceilings, all the reverence
of eighteenth century religious fervor
and juggling these rows of cells
where the Coahuiltecans lived

who labored in praise of a God
they were just beginning to know,
one who surely loved the Franciscans
more than He loved them.

Today the missions stretching out from San Antonio
leave the Alamo mid-city
where pumpkin-shaped carriages
carry tourists through adjacent streets.

Today big buses with smoked windows
spill visitors by the hundreds
who follow their tour guides from courtyards
to naves, marvel at the math

of an *acequia* still watering ancient fields,
restoration of a working flour mill,
its perfect powder
soft between their fingers.

You tell me you were married in this church
decades before it was a National Park.
I aim my camera
and the wedding comes into view,

torrential rains flood the building
and you an hour late
to the ceremony.
Four hundred crowd inside,

to escape the downpour, prelude
to a life of creativity and fertile love
where good crops grow
despite the drought.

Memory of that day echoes in the pulse
that linked Indian slaves
to their Franciscan masters,
and loops around that other place

where you learned to read by searching
for meaning in the dirty word
that stopped your mother
mid-Huckleberry Finn.

Book-lover's heart on your sleeve,
you sang your way
from west Texas to Prague
and back,

straddle the liberation of this theology,
where every byway poses a question
you can answer or have fun trying.
Coahuiltecans stand in solemn witness.

Giving Nothing Back

She holds the mirror
but sees nothing.
No image past its glittering surface,
blinding as sun.

She combs fingers
through disobeying strands of hair
threatening her left eye,
dark mole nudging her ear.

Her right temple, too tender
for caress, echoes the toe
of a man's boot:
the memory that will not fade.

Centuries stand between her
and that death.
One small drum of skin
repelling touch

and an empty mirror
withholding answers,
sucking image,
giving nothing back.

Lips Long Since Returned to Forest Mulch

The Maya wrote their concept of zero
as a resting oval with small curved lines,
one on top two at the bottom,
coming together in points at either end.
Three shorter lines
rise within like eyelashes or tiny sails.

The glyph is a leaf, a seed, an eye but not only.
Something about the image escapes
when I approach,
hides in a region I will never see.
Imagination loses me
in canyons of mossy stone.

Hull and sails gone to secret
in a place so inland from oceans
outlier to deciphering minds
centuries before sailing vessels
crossed our horizons:
symbol of emptiness filled.

Pale blue washes my dream
and that glyph invites me
into its home.
I am both eager and afraid.
When I enter my skin glistens
with gold dust oblivious to market worth.

Expressing zero, the Maya didn't mean nothing,
an idea that baffled Europeans
as late as the renaissance.

A void neither native to its vigesimal place
nor absence
waiting for something to happen.

Like the dot representing one
or bar claiming five,
this small basket boat had its work cut out
along the Long Count
or Calendar Round:
endless legacies of birth and death.

In my dream there is always someone
I know well
and someone I meet for the first time.
Familiarity and fear
shoot their arrows
into the six regions of my heart.

They etch themselves on my skin like Nazi numbers
or tracer flares from dictates
claiming to comfort those
taught to believe that wars end war,
our love is unnatural, learning isn't for girls
or some humans prefer poverty.

I ask myself if mathematical brilliance
kept the Maya safe from storms,
fed crops or helped cacao beans
journey from tree to rich brown liquid
filling clay mugs
raised to lips long since returned to forest mulch.

We are drawn to examine a weighted base
and three flickers of hope.
I want to reach out and take this zero
between my fingers' broken feathers,

follow its burning light to questions
unanswered then and now.

Until we inhale the air they breathed
into our own lungs,
unless we can feel what they felt
walking toward the sacrificial bench,
the code may be broken and broken again
but will resist letting us in.

Our Customs

Recoil at humans eating humans, *cannibal*
a word that holds repulsion in its craw
even when speaking of a people
whose culture eludes us
through today's myopic prism.

Evidence of boiling human skulls in pots
unearthed at Ancestral Puebloan sites
brings science to philosophical assumption.
Judge not, lest you be judged
the wise man said, but they cannot judge

who are safely dead. Neither titillation
nor indignation grab my heart,
intent and circumstance germane
to what we believe and how we proceed
upon this grieving land.

I prefer to think about chocolate making
its addictive way from purple pods
on Andean lowland trees,
moving along Xochimilco's waterways,
from the stones of Tenochtitlán and Teotihuácan,

stopping to rest at Guachimontones and Paquimé,
carried in salivating bags, its aroma escaping
their loose weaves, grated into those same
clay pots, mixed with maize or spring water
deep in the alcove at Kiet Seel.

With a diet of corn and squash and beans,
occasional deer or rabbit and rare luxury
of nuts, the dark delight must have been
reserved for feasts that marked birth,
death, coming of age or victory in war.

Mexico's Cora people trace the origin of *chile*
to a long-ago banquet where a man,
brave in those acts where men excel,
wiped sweat from his genitals, brought fingers
to lips and tasted the world's first hot sauce.

I bring my fingers to eager lips, taste chocolate
two millennia before Black Forest Cake,
perfect éclair, Godiva, or Dairy Queen Soft-Serve,
when seed and pod and root still held the poetry
of breath and tongue in magical embrace.

Ten centuries beyond that residue of bone on clay
and chocolate's journey north,
we humans still devour one another
in ways I do not wish to honor in a poem
nor will I place our customs above theirs.

Our Imperfect History

Clinging to old wood gracing storm-rocked shallows
the bivalve gives no outer sign of life.
In its world: our imperfect history
from the memory of that artist's hand
on the cave wall in southern France
to the unborn whose mind already considers
kindness a problem to be solved.

My ancestor defies current and encroachment.
Even in her primitive state
she knows tenacity is the greater virtue,
loyalty always welcome when water bubbles dark
and murky. Simplicity quenches thirst.
An explosion of chemosensory cells
jewel the night, then slowly fall to quiet.

I need not speak to the mollusk of separation,
irreparable pain, those I was forced
to leave behind or that train
arriving minutes after the ghost woman departs.
I am not made to retrieve the beginning
of this number sequence strung out in despair
or finger the beads on any rosary.

Spent, exhausted, tired to death with calling
on our brilliant minds to solve the agonies
of these or any other times,
I turn to the truly organic among us:
filter feeder, mantle, simple eyes.
I ask the question that has no answer
and wait to be welcomed home.

Perfect Makeup and Convincing Fear

Better than embedded journalism
or the latest video game:
reality make-believe, live bullets
and a chance to watch celebrities
risk death for superior ratings.

They join Navy Seals, out of work
Green Berets, ex Marine sergeants,
invisible Delta Force
mercenaries:
heroes all.

Commanded by General Wesley Clark
who once aspired to be president
on an anti-war platform
back when public opinion
favored peace.

They're calling it *Stars Earn Stripes*
in perfect makeup
and convincing fear.
Nothing like it
has ever been screened before.

The ultimate real entertainment
until even the danger of death
is not enough
and the studio hacks devise a way
to suck the addicted into the action.

At This Crossroads

Stone against stone, hand tool
on rock wall, she scraped
and thought about what she would say
to those she would never know.

I presume a consciousness
of future, when
she might have been announcing
water here

or *go beyond this point*
only at your peril.
The grain tastes better this season
in the broad delta at her feet.

Thin light of early morning, sun
pushes through soft leaves,
warms her skin, pulls temperature
inside out.

She cuts one vertical line
beside three circles, crosses them
with two mountain ridges
and a shy moon.

Deep in distant future
a freight train sounds in city night,
its wail rises
to greet her where she works.

Then another and another,
the going-wail
and sharper coming-tone,
all night from the four directions

where past and future meet
at this crossroads on the land.

I and *Am*

Kike, nigger, greaser, injun, chink,
 slut, faggot, dyke: ugly words
bloated by fear and ignorance
strut the streets again these days,
greedy and shameless.

Meanwhile *I* and *am* huddle together,
hoping no one separates their fragile bodies.
Longer words take refuge in crowds,
confident numbers will keep them safe
or give them leverage.

We hear rumors of a renegade colony
where deceitful words
flood the market with counterfeit:
American exceptionalism, melting pot,
nation-building, democracy.

And we resist. *I am. You are. We are,*
open our tired hearts,
retrieve those battered books,
welcome the brave words home,
let memory in.

Some insist: *Sticks and stones will break my bones*
but words will never hurt me:
Don't make me laugh. Or cry.
Banned words ban history, banned history
bans memory. Life withers and dies.

So *I* and *am* twin up for the long haul,
cling to each other in dignity,
victims of every injustice

beyond those empty stand-ins
meant to bring us all down.

For all those books that saved our lives,
the clandestine words are ready
to come out of hiding and nurture our children.
Let us tend the safe houses,
leave fresh water along the trail.

Identity Bursts its Seams

Time grew thin for me
and I could see clear through it
to the other side.

I rubbed its airy prism
between finger pads
a million questions have worn clean.

No traces remain
for those who pride themselves
on cunning or deception.

Still, identity bursts its seems
all up and down this skin
holding every rise and hollow of my age.

I close my eyes and each time I pass go
wait for reassurance
it was worth the risk.

Not This Life

If my family had stayed in that New York suburb
never ventured cross-country
in the old black Studebaker
to mountains that glow with pink
with a last burst of sun each afternoon.

If I hadn't found my mentors or they me, words
moving in my blood like calving glaciers,
I disappeared into Rothko's painting
and the father of poetry smiled
and asked me to read my young poem aloud.

If I hadn't scorned hypocrisy, given birth alone,
crossed borders where wars raged
and found all those Davids
with slingshots on alert, laughed
when another language bit my lips.

Ghosts come at any hour, take my hand,
weave memory from strands of human hair.
If strangers if lovers if those
we least expected to survive.
I follow the lines on my own map.

If you hadn't walked into that classroom
purple overalls yellow sneakers
willing to take a chance
and twenty-six years later still in love.
If you hadn't I hadn't we hadn't

life would have happened, just not this life.

My Question

I wanted to know which question
had my name on it,
the one
belonging only to me,
the one I could hold apart.

I had some clues about ownership
learned to study products,
effective advertising,
where the convoluted byways led
and where the prizes hid.

I was always afraid when
Mother left the room
and between the wooden slats
of my crib
all I could see was sunlight,

stuffed animals
with the wrong color eyes,
fake skin,
absence of temperature
and mouths requiring ventriloquist skill.

I always excelled at telling
the expected lies
and also those drawing punishment:
suffocating choke chain
of invisible magnets.

I kept my fear list up to date:
fear of the dark forest,
of anything that grew too quickly,
Grandpa's dreamy eyes
and con man's smile.

My grandpa took ordinary words
and turned them into toadstools,
poison dripping
between my little girl lips,
entering undefended openings.

Grandma stood behind him
quiet and watching
until she could be sure
stop and go
were safely out of sight.

And all this time I looked
for my question,
the one that belonged
to me alone, memory
of the bison's muscled shoulder

or line of running horses painted
on the walls of a cave
32,000 years ago.
A question I could spend
the rest of my life answering.

The fields where I searched
turned desolate.
Was this the right lens, a language
that would cooperate?
Years passed, decades and lovers,

children and their children,
wars and poems.
Grandpa and Grandma died
inauspicious deaths
in a century I struggle to remember.

And I have found my question,
the one that belongs to me alone.
It cradles me through waning nights
and makes itself scarce
when the FBI comes knocking at my door.

I would tell you what it is
but then—you know—
I would have to kill you.

Colophon

Helvetica, Bodoni or Arial Black uncurl
in the colophon of this gem-like book.
How the poem inhabits the page,
its sounds and silences standing proud.

One last chance to make sure the reader
spends a moment contemplating form
as well as content, listens for
barely audible breath or hard U turn.

Form and content: two wings of a bird
who carries my heart in its sharp beak,
pulls it to where surprise or shock
shatters the mirror I hide behind my back.

Perfect colophon: careful prescription
or serious warning, country cousin
to the main characters, embodied spirits
who steal center stage, demand my attention.

Read to the book's final page, feel its weight
in both hands. Breathe
the vegetable scent of inks
and know this: every letter counts.

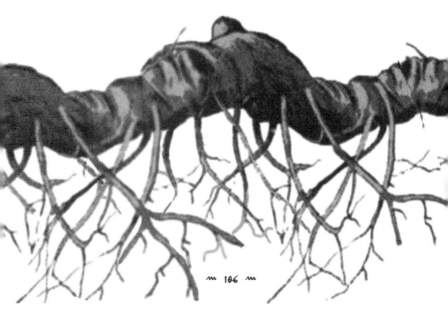

Acknowledgments

Some of these poems, sometimes in slightly different versions, first appeared in *Adobe Walls*, *Beatlick Press Anthology*, *Caesura*, *The Café Review*, *Huizache*, *Malpais Review*, *The Más Tequila Review*, *So It Goes*, "*The Sunday Poem*" in *The Duke City Fix,* and *The Rag.* I also want to acknowledge Naropa University's wonderful Summer Writing Program, where I have taught in recent years. Cultural Rhizomes and Intentional Communities was the theme of the program's second week in the summer of 2012. This inspired my thinking about rhizomes and, ultimately, many of the poems included in this book.

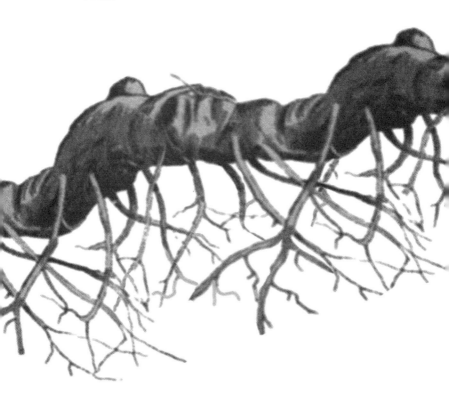

About the Author

Margaret Randall is a feminist poet, writer, photographer and social activist. She is the author of over 100 books. Born in New York City in 1936, she has lived for extended periods in Albuquerque, New York, Seville, Mexico City, Havana, and Managua. Shorter stays in Peru and North Vietnam were also formative. In the 1960s with Sergio Mondragón, she co-founded and co-edited *El Corno Emplumado / The Plumed Horn,* a bilingual literary journal which for eight years published some of the most dynamic and meaningful writing of an era. From 1984 through 1994 she taught at a number of U.S. universities.

Randall was privileged to live among New York's abstract expressionists in the 1950s and early '60s, participate in the Mexican student movement of 1968, share important years of the Cuban revolution (1969-1980), the first four years of Nicaragua's Sandinista project (1980-1984), and visit North Vietnam during the heroic last months of the U.S. American war in that country (1974). Her four children—Gregory, Sarah, Ximena and Ana—have given her ten grandchildren. She has lived with her life companion, the painter and teacher Barbara Byers, for the past quarter century.

Upon her return to the United States from Nicaragua in 1984, Randall was ordered to be deported when the government invoked the 1952 McCarran-Walter Immigration and Nationality Act, judging opinions expressed in some of her books to be "against the good order and happiness of the United States." The Center for Constitutional Rights defended Randall, and many writers and others joined in an almost five-year battle for reinstatement of citizenship. She won her case in 1989.

In 1990 Randall was awarded the Lillian Hellman and Dashiell Hammett grant for writers victimized by political repression. In 2004 she was the first recipient of PEN New Mexico's Dorothy Doyle Lifetime Achievement Award for Writing and Human Rights Activism.

To Change the World: My Life in Cuba, was recently published by Rutgers University Press. "The Unapologetic Life of Margaret Randall" is an hour-long documentary by Minneapolis filmmakers Lu Lippold and Pam Colby. It is distributed by Cinema Guild in New York City.

Randall's most recent collections of poetry and photographs are *Their Backs to the Sea* (2009) and *My Town: A Memoir of Albuquerque, New Mexico* (2010), *As If the Empty Chair: Poems for the disappeared / Como si la silla vacía: Poemas para los desaparecidos* (2011) and *Where Do We Go From Here?* (2012), all published by Wings Press. For more information about the author, visit her website at www.margaretrandall.org.

WINGS PRESS

Colophon

This first edition of *The Rhizome as a Field of Broken Bones*, by Margaret Randall, has been printed on 55 pound EB "natural" paper containing a percentage of recycled fiber. Book titles are set in Pablo type, the text in Minion type. This book was designed by Bryce Milligan.

On-line catalogue and ordering available at
www.wingspress.com

Wings Press titles are distributed to the trade by the
Independent Publishers Group
www.ipgbook.com
and in Europe by
www.gazellebookservices.co.uk

Also available as an ebook.